Taking A.D.D. To School

A "School" Story About Attention Deficit Disorder

MALLINCKRODT

A D H D

A CONCENTRATED EFFORT

If It's Mallinckrodt, It's Under Control™

MALLINCKRODT

Published by
JayJo Books, L.L.C.
Publishing Special Books for Special Kids®
P.O. Box 213
Valley Park, MO 63088-0213

Edited by Kim Gosselin
Designed by Tom Dineen

Library of Congress Cataloging-in-Publication Data
Weiner, Ellen
Taking A.D.D. to School/Ellen Weiner - Special Edition - Third Printing
Library of Congress Catalog Card Number 99-71578
1. Juvenile/Non-Fiction/Children's Literature
2. Health Education
3. A.D.D./A.D.H.D.
4. Children's Disabilities
ISBN 1-891383-06-X
Library of Congress
4th book in our *"Special Kids in School"*® series.

The opinions expressed in Taking A.D.D. to School are those solely of the author. A.D.D./A.D.H.D. care is highly individualized. One should never alter medical care without **first** consulting their own physician.

JayJo Books, L.L.C.
Publishing Special Books for Special Kids®
P.O. Box 213
Valley Park, MO 63088-0213

Dedication

Dedicated to the memory of my husband, Sheldon K. Weiner, whose tragic death has propelled me to explore new and exciting areas in my life.

Hi boys and girls!

My name is Ben. I'm eight years old. I like playing basketball. I'm also a kid living with Attention Deficit/Hyperactivity Disorder. For short, it's called A.D.D.

Sometimes I do things without even thinking about them. There are times when I can't seem to sit still, even for a minute. Kids with A.D.D. seem to have even more trouble sitting still and paying attention in school.

Nobody can catch A.D.D. from *anyone!* Kids that have it though (like me), can take special medicines. The special medicines might help us feel better and help us find it easier to pay attention.

I am in the third grade now. I found out that I had A.D.D. last year when I was in second grade. Lots of things went wrong when I was in second grade...

In second grade I had to start learning to sit quietly at my own desk. I tried really hard to do my work, but there were just too many other things to look at.

I tried to pay attention, but sometimes my teachers didn't think I was. I couldn't remember what I was supposed to do. A lot of times, I would raise my hand and ask my teachers to tell me again what they had said.

They were always saying, "Ben, pay attention," or "Ben, try to concentrate!"

ometimes I couldn't help myself from doing certain things. When my teacher asked a question, I would yell out the answer before I even knew what he was going to ask. My teacher got kind of angry when I did this.

He called it "disrupting" the class.

econd grade was when I started to learn a special kind of writing called cursive. We had to practice it everyday. No matter what I did, I couldn't get the letters to look like the ones on the big chart hanging above the chalkboard. It was even hard for me to read it!

I couldn't keep my desk neat, either. Papers were always getting crumbled up or folded. My pencils always fell on the floor. I couldn't even keep my notebook in order!

very afternoon at school we had quiet time. This was the time when everyone was supposed to look at books, finish up their work, or just rest. This was the hardest time of all for me. I *wanted* to do what the teacher said, but I couldn't stop talking or jumping out of my seat. This got me in a lot of trouble.

A few times I even had to go to the principal's office!

I always loved recess because it was the one time I could run around and have fun. I liked to play with the other kids. But sometimes they wouldn't let me join in. I felt sad. The other kids said it was because I never wanted to wait my turn.

I couldn't help it.

chool wasn't fun anymore...the teachers all said they couldn't "control" me. The kids didn't want to play with me. Everything was getting so mixed up. I could hear people talking to me, but I couldn't always understand what they were saying. I felt so bad, that my mom took me to the doctor for a check-up.

It turned out to be the best check-up I ever had!

y doctor and some of the nurses asked me a lot of questions. A few days later we had a big meeting. The doctor said that I had something called A.D.D.

The doctor gave me some special medicine to try to help me feel better and to do better in school.

 little while after I started taking the special medicine, I felt a lot better! It was like when you're watching television: Sometimes the picture gets all fuzzy and then all of a sudden it becomes very clear. It was like seeing everything with brand new eyes!

I was able to pay attention in class. I even won the cursive writing award one month!!

he doctor said that I may not have to take my special medicine forever.

I visit my doctor and nurses a lot. I can talk to them about my feelings. They are my friends. I can tell them how much better I feel at school. I'm feeling a lot better at home now, too!

hird grade is just great! I'm having so much fun in school this year. My teachers always tell me how proud they are of my behavior.

It feels good to hear that! Now my A.D.D. doesn't stop me from doing anything I'm supposed to do. After all, a lot of kids have A.D.D. just like me. I'm not the only one!

To order additional copies of <u>Taking A.D.D. to School</u> contact your local bookstore or library. Or call the publisher directly at (636) 861-1331. Please visit our website for further information at: **www.jayjo.com!** E-mail us at **jayjobooks@aol.com!**

Write to us at:
JayJo Books, L.L.C.
P.O. Box 213
Valley Park, MO 63088-0213

Look for other books including:
From our *Special Kids in School®* series:
<u>Taking Diabetes to School</u>
<u>Taking Asthma to School</u>
<u>Taking Seizure Disorders to School</u>
<u>Taking Food Allergies to School</u>
<u>Taking Cerebral Palsy to School</u>
<u>Taking Cystic Fibrosis to School</u>
And others coming soon!
Others Available Now!
<u>SPORTSercise!</u>
A "School" Story about
Exercise-Induced Asthma
<u>Taking Asthma to Camp</u>
A Fictional Story about Asthma Camp
<u>ZooAllergy</u>
A Fun Story about Allergy
and Asthma Triggers
<u>Rufus Comes Home</u>
Rufus The Bear With Diabetes™
<u>The ABC's of Asthma</u>
An Asthma Alphabet Book
for Kids of All Ages
<u>Taming the Diabetes Dragon</u>
A Fictional Story about Living Well with Diabetes

<u>Trick-or-Treat for Diabetes</u>
A Halloween Story for Kids Living with Diabetes
And our first large hardcover book
<u>Smoking STINKS!!</u>®
A Fictional Story about the Many Ways Smoking "Stinks"!!
From our new *Substance Free Kids®* series.

A portion of the profits from this book is donated to CHADD, Children & Adults with Attention-Deficit Hyperactivity Disorder.